BUDGETING FOR BEGINNERS

A COLLECTION OF OVER 60+ TEMPLATES!

A WARM

WELCOME

DEAR READER,

Congratulations on making the decision to take control of your financial destiny! Whether you're looking to build a stable foundation, invest wisely, or achieve specific financial goals, rest assured that this workbook was created to support and guide you every step of the way.

I am honored that you chose this book to guide you on this journey , and I can't wait to witness the incredible growth and achievements that lie ahead. If there's anything you need, please don't hesitate to reach out by emailing jennaastillman@gmail.com.

Here's to a prosperous and rewarding financial future!

Warm regards,

Jenna Stillman

CONTENTS

BUDGETING FOR BEGINNERS

SECTION 1

INTRODUCTION

INTRO

Raise your hand if the word "budget" stresses you out! If you're slowly raising your hand, you shouldn't feel ashamed. Budgeting stresses everyone out. That reason alone is why roughly 68% of Americans don't utilize one. When we think about budgeting, most often we think of extreme restriction. However, it doesn't (and shouldn't) be that way. If that was truly the only way, absolutely no one would follow through with it.

Budgeting does **NOT** have to be restrictive, it does **NOT** have to take up hours of your day and it does **NOT** require you to have a degree in finance. Budgeting can be easy and extremely beneficial, especially if you understand the logic behind the process and create a healthy money relationship along the way.

So, here's the deal.

If you want to be successful with budgeting, you need to understand that budgeting **HAS** to look more like creating a <u>spending plan</u> vs. <u>eliminating</u> the things that are not essential. The goal should be to create lasting change by making long term decisions, not get rid of all the nonessential things ASAP. Most people fail at budgeting because they aim for complete restriction, which is **not sustainable**. It's all about balance, and what do you need to assure that you can pay your mortgage while still taking full advantage of Taco Tuesday? **A PLAN**.

This workbook will help you get ahead with your finances without giving up everything that makes you happy. Because what's the purpose of working hard if you can't spend your money to **LOVE** your life?

THE POSITIVE MONEY MINDSET

It's important to understand how YOU feel about money and how those feelings may affect your beliefs. Someone who is confident with money has certain positive mindset qualities that enable them to make informed and effective financial decisions!

Here are some of those qualities:

Financial Literacy: Confident individuals have a good understanding of financial concepts, terms, and strategies. They are familiar with budgeting, investing, saving, and debt management, which helps them make informed decisions.

Goal Setting: They set clear financial goals for themselves, whether short-term or long-term. These goals serve as a roadmap, helping them allocate resources and make decisions that align with their objectives.

Long-Term Thinking: Confident individuals focus on the big picture and think about the long-term implications of their financial choices. They are less likely to be swayed by short-term trends or impulsive decisions.

Adaptability: They are adaptable and open to adjusting their financial strategies as circumstances change. This might involve shifting investment allocations, adjusting budgets, or changing saving strategies as needed.

Patience: Confident individuals understand that building wealth takes time and are patient with their investment strategies. They don't chase get-rich-quick schemes but instead focus on consistent, disciplined approaches.

Self-Discipline: They have the self-discipline to stick to their financial plans and avoid unnecessary spending. This helps them stay on track toward their goals and avoid impulsive decisions.

Financial Awareness: Confident individuals stay informed about their financial situation. They regularly review their accounts, track spending, and monitor investments to ensure they are on track to meet their goals.

Openness to Learning: They are willing to learn from their mistakes and seek out new information. They continuously educate themselves about personal finance and investment opportunities.

Emotional Intelligence: They are aware of their emotions and how they can impact financial decisions. They make efforts to separate emotions from financial choices, reducing the likelihood of impulsive actions driven by feelings.

Resilience: Confident individuals can bounce back from financial setbacks and setbacks. They don't let failures define them, but instead, they learn from their experiences and adapt their strategies.

Contentment: They have a healthy relationship with money and understand that financial success doesn't solely determine their self-worth. Confident individuals find contentment in their financial achievements without constantly chasing more.

Giving Back: They are generous and understand the importance of giving back. Confident individuals are more likely to engage in philanthropic activities and help others with their financial knowledge.

What positive money mindset(s) do you already excel at?

THE NEGATIVE MONEY MINDSET

When it comes to money, people often experience a wide range of mindset struggles that can impact their financial decisions and overall well-being.

Here are some common mindset struggles related to money:

Comparison Trap: Constantly comparing one's financial situation to others can lead to feelings of inadequacy, jealousy, and low self-esteem. This mindset can drive people to overspend to keep up appearances or make choices that aren't aligned with their true financial goals.

Instant Gratification: The desire for immediate pleasure or satisfaction can lead to impulsive spending and a lack of long-term financial planning. This mindset can hinder savings and investment efforts.

Lack of Financial Literacy: Insufficient knowledge about personal finance can lead to poor decision-making, confusion, and susceptibility to financial scams. This mindset struggle can be overcome through education and seeking advice from trusted sources.

Emotional Spending: Using shopping or spending as a way to cope with emotions such as stress, sadness, or boredom can lead to overspending and financial instability.

Keeping Up with Lifestyle Inflation: As income increases, some people might increase their spending to match the new level of income, rather than saving or investing the surplus. This can hinder wealth-building efforts.

Debt Apathy: Some individuals normalize debt and don't see it as a problem, leading to a cycle of accumulating more debt without a plan to pay it off. This mindset can hinder financial progress and increase stress over time.

Perfectionism: Striving for perfection in financial decisions can lead to paralysis and indecision. This mindset can prevent individuals from taking action on important financial matters.

Lack of Goal Setting: Without clear financial goals, individuals might struggle to prioritize spending, saving, and investing. Setting specific, achievable goals can provide a sense of direction and motivation.
Overconfidence: Believing one has a better grasp of financial matters than they actually do can lead to risky investments and poor financial decisions.

Neglecting Self-Worth: Associating self-worth solely with financial success can lead to feelings of inadequacy if financial goals aren't met. It's important to recognize that one's value goes beyond monetary achievements.

Ignoring Retirement Planning: Many people delay or neglect planning for retirement, assuming they have plenty of time. Starting early is crucial for building a sufficient nest egg.

Reluctance to Seek Help: Some individuals avoid seeking financial advice or assistance due to pride or embarrassment. However, seeking help from financial professionals can provide valuable insights and strategies.

What negative money mindset(s) do you need to work on?

MONEY MINDSET

Maintaining a healthy relationship with money involves self-reflection, awareness, and a proactive approach to managing your finances. Here are some questions you can ask yourself to assess and improve your relationship with money:

WHAT ARE MY FINANCIAL GOALS?

- *Do I have clear short-term and long-term financial goals?*
- *Are my goals realistic and achievable?*
- *Am I actively working toward my goals?*

HOW DO I FEEL ABOUT MONEY?

- *Do I feel stressed or anxious when thinking about money?*
- *Do I associate my self-worth with my financial status?*
- *Am I comfortable discussing money matters with others?*

WHAT IS MY APPROACH TO BUDGETING AND SPENDING?

- *Do I have a budget in place to track my income and expenses?*
- *Am I spending within my means or consistently overspending?*
- *Do I differentiate between needs and wants when making spending decisions?*

HOW DO I HANDLE DEBT?

- *Am I managing my debt effectively and making timely payments?*
- *Do I understand the interest rates and terms of my debts?*
- *Am I taking steps to reduce and eventually eliminate my debt?*

MONEY MINDSET

WHAT IS MY ATTITUDE TOWARD SAVINGS AND INVESTMENTS?

- *Am I saving a portion of my income regularly?*
- *Have I started investing for the future?*
- *Do I understand different investment options and their associated risks?*

AM I PRACTICING FINANCIAL SELF-CARE?

- *Do I give myself permission to enjoy reasonable and planned purchases?*
- *Am I setting aside money for leisure and personal enjoyment?*
- *Do I balance my financial responsibilities with self-care needs?*

HOW DO I RESPOND TO FINANCIAL SETBACKS?

- *How do I react when facing unexpected expenses or financial challenges?*
- *Am I prepared with an emergency fund to handle unexpected situations?*

AM I CONTINUOUSLY LEARNING ABOUT PERSONAL FINANCE?

- *Do I actively seek out information about personal finance and financial literacy?*
- *Am I open to learning from my financial mistakes and successes?*

MONEY MINDSET

DO I SEEK PROFESSIONAL FINANCIAL ADVICE?

- *Have I consulted with financial advisors or professionals for guidance?*
- *Do I seek help when making major financial decisions?*

DO I PRACTICE GRATITUDE AND CONTENTMENT?

- *Do I appreciate my current financial situation while working toward improvement?*
- *Do I find joy in non-monetary aspects of life?*
- *Am I content with my financial achievements without constantly comparing myself to others?*

AM I GIVING BACK AND BEING GENEROUS?

- *Do I engage in charitable activities or donate to causes I care about?*
- *Do I prioritize helping others with my financial knowledge and resources?*

AM I IN CONTROL OF MY FINANCIAL DECISIONS?

- *Do I make conscious choices aligned with my values and goals?*
- *Am I avoiding impulsive spending and decisions driven by emotions?*

OPTIMIZE VS. SACRIFICE

Using optimization with your monthly budget involves finding ways to make the most of your available resources and expenses without necessarily making significant sacrifices or feeling deprived. By adopting a strategic approach, you can maximize the value you get from your budget while still enjoying a reasonable level of comfort and satisfaction.

OPTIMIZATION

- ✓ Shop smart
- ✓ Cut down on unnecessary costs
- ✓ Negotiate bills and contracts
- ✓ Plan for occasional outings in advance and set aside funds
- ✓ Review and adjust regularly

SACRIFICE

WHAT TO AVOID

- X Spend the absolute least amount of money possible
- X Say "no" to all extracurricular spending
- X Feel guilt and shame when spending
- X Miss out on unique opportunities
- X Never review or adjust

IMAGINE YOUR LIFE IS

PICTURE PERFECT

"What would you attempt to do if you knew you could not fail?" -Robert Schiller

QUESTIONS:	WRITE YOUR ANSWERS HERE
What does your "dream life" look like? Where are you living? What are you driving? How are you spending your time?	
What would you need to accomplish for you to feel like you had a "successful" life?	
What non-tangable things bring you the most happiness?	

THINK ABOUT THIS

Congratulations! You just won the lottery!

You have 100 million dollars to spend before you die. What are you spending the next 10 years doing?

Now that you have done and seen it all, how are you going to spend your free time? What is truly going to bring you the most peace, joy, and satisfaction?

How can you do that thing without winning the lottery?

WHEEL OF LIFE

The wheel of life is a visual tool used to assess and determine how balanced your life is. You start off by determining each area of your life (these can be the most important areas of your life and the roles you have) and mark these out on the wheel below. Evaluate each category and score from 1 to 5 (1 being the lowest) and then connect the dots.

DATE

SCORE

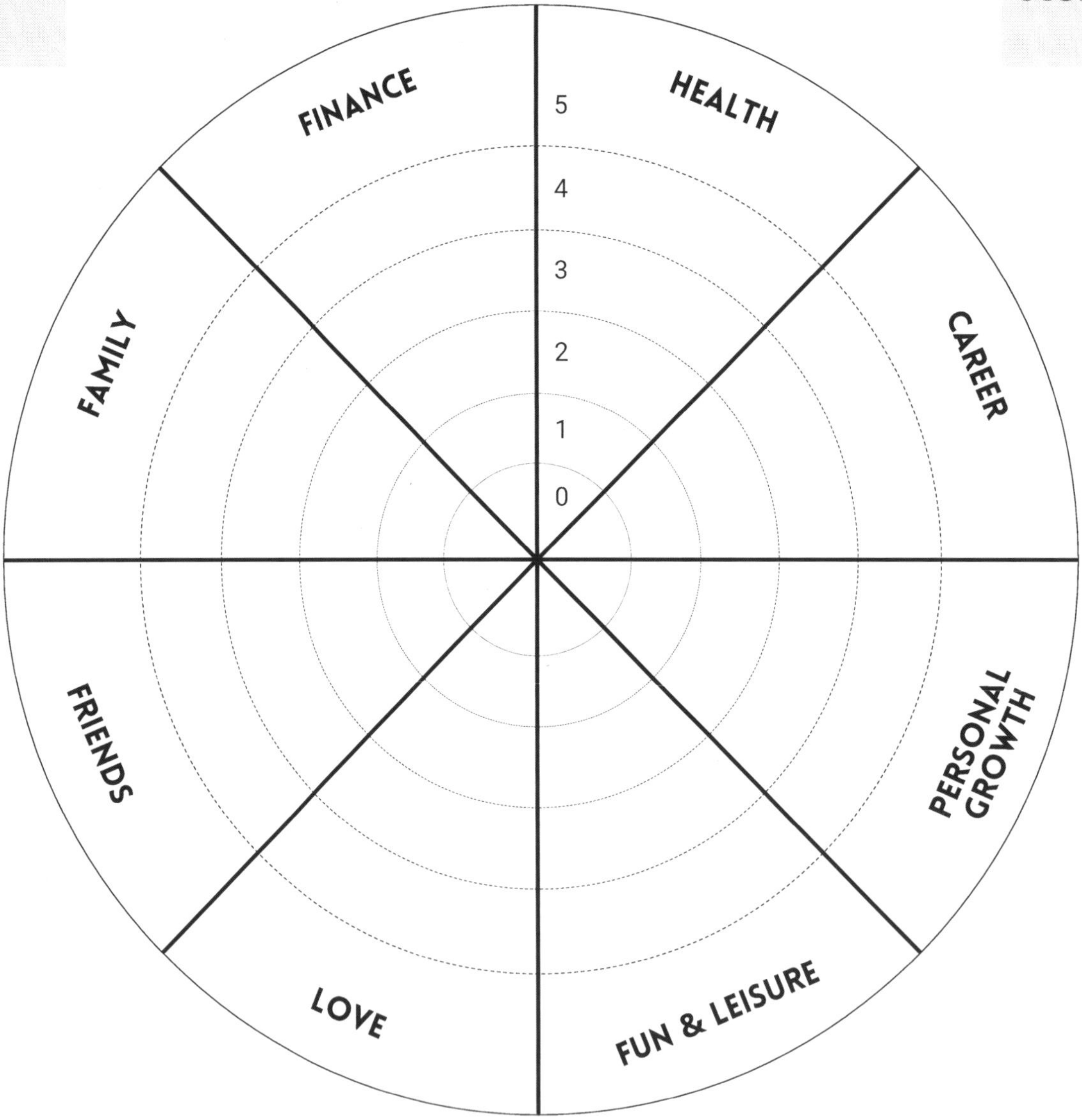

YOU CAN DO THIS EXERCISE BEFORE AND AFTER YOU IMPLEMENT CHANGES TO SEE HOW YOUR SCORES HAVE IMPROVED!

SECTION 2

ASSESSMENT

ASSETS

Assets are economic resources or valuable possessions owned by an individual that have measurable value. These resources can be tangible, such as physical items like real estate, vehicles, or machinery, or intangible, such as financial investments, patents, or copyrights.

CASH & BANK ACCOUNTS

Checking, Savings & Cash

REAL ESTATE

Home, Rental Properties or Land

INVESTMENTS

Stocks, Bonds, Mutual Funds

VEHICLES

Cars, Motorcycles or Recreational Vehicles

PERSONAL PROPERTY

Electronics, Jewelry & Valuables

RETIREMENT

401K, IRA

ASSETS

Current assets *are the assets that are expected to be used up or converted into cash within a short time frame, often within a year.* ***Fixed assets****, on the other hand, are assets that are held for the long term and are not intended for quick conversion into cash.*

COLLECTIBLES

Art, Antiques, Stamps, Coins

INTELLECTUAL PROPERTY

Copyrights, Patents & Trademarks

HOME EQUITY

The portion of your home value that you own outright

CRYPTOCURRENC Y

Bitcoin, Ethereum

CASH VALUE LIFE INSURANCE

The cash value component of permanent life insurance policies

OTHER

LIABILITIES

Liabilities are financial obligations or debts that one owes to other parties. They represent the claims or responsibilities that must be fulfilled by providing assets, services, or payments in the future.

	HOME	AMOUNT
1	RENT/ MORTGAGE	$
2	HOME INSURANCE/HOA	$
3	UTILITIES (WATER, GAS, ELECTRIC)	$
4	TV & INTERNET	$
5	OUTDOOR/GARDEN	$
6	HOME REPAIRS	$
7		$
8		$
9		$

LIABILITIES

VEHICLE	AMOUNT
1 CAR PAYMENT	$
2 INSURANCE	$
3 GAS	$
4 MAINTENANCE	$
5	$
6	$
7	$
8	$
9	$

LIABILITIES

MEDICAL	AMOUNT
1 DOCTOR	$
2 DENTIST	$
3 EYECARE/CONTACTS	$
4 MEDICATION	$
5 SPA TREATMENT	$
6	$
7	$
8	$
9	$

LIABILITIES

FOOD	AMOUNT
1 GROCERIES	$
2 EATING OUT	$
3 FOOD SUBSCRIPTIONS	$
4 COFFEE	$
5	$
6	$
7	$
8	$
9	$

LIABILITIES

LIFE	AMOUNT
1 CHILD CARE/SUPPORT	$
2 BEAUTY/SKINCARE	$
3 CLOTHING	$
4 ENTERTAINMENT	$
5 GIFTS	$
6 SUBSCRIPTIONS	$
7	$
8	$
9	$

LIABILITIES

DEBT	AMOUNT
1 CREDIT CARD #1	$
2 CREDIT CARD #2	$
3 CREDIT CARD #3	$
4 STUDENT LOAN/ TUITION	$
5 LOAN #1	$
6 LOAN #2	$
7	$
8	$
9	$

LIABILITIES/ TOTALS

OTHER	AMOUNT
1	$
2	$
3	$
4	$
5	$

1 HOME TOTAL	$
2 VEHICLE TOTAL	$
3 MEDICAL TOTAL	$
4 FOOD TOTAL	$
5 LIFE TOTAL	$

TOTAL LIABILITIES =

QUESTIONS

Regular budget reviews help you track your spending, identify areas where you might be overspending, and ensure that you're staying within your financial goals. It's a proactive way to catch any issues early, make informed decisions, and keep your financial plans aligned with your objectives, ultimately helping you achieve better financial stability and success.

	YES	NO	MAYBE
Do I have a budget in place?	☐	☐	☐
Am I tracking my expenses regularly?	☐	☐	☐
Do I spend within my budget?	☐	☐	☐
Do I review my bank/credit card statements?	☐	☐	☐
Am I contributing to savings & investments?	☐	☐	☐
Am I impulse buying?	☐	☐	☐
Do I differentiate between needs and wants?	☐	☐	☐
Am I taking advantage of coupons & discounts?	☐	☐	☐
Do I have an emergency fund?	☐	☐	☐
Am I paying off my credit cards in full?	☐	☐	☐
Am I making thoughtful purchases?	☐	☐	☐

WHAT IS YOUR

NET WORTH

Net Worth = Total Assets- Total Liabilities
Net worth is the value that remains when you subtract all debts and obligations from the total value of everything you own. Net worth is often used as an indicator of overall financial health and wealth.

DATE ____________

TOTAL ASSETS	TOTAL LIABILITIES	NET WORTH

DATE ____________

TOTAL ASSETS	TOTAL LIABILITIES	NET WORTH

GOAL SETTING

SMART goals promote accountability and motivate you to take purposeful actions. They increase the likelihood of achieving desired outcomes!

S

SPECIFIC: What do you want to achieve?

M

MEASURABLE: How will you know when you have reached your goal?

A

ACHIEVABLE: Is the goal within your power to accomplish?

R

REALISTIC: Can you realistically achieve your goal?

T

TIME-BOUND: When do you want to achieve your goal by?

GOAL SETTING

GOAL 1 :	Why it's important :	
	Measurable Outcome :	

GOAL 2 :	Why it's important :	
	Measurable Outcome :	

GOAL 3 :	Why it's important :	
	Measurable Outcome :	

REMEMBER TO KEEP YOUR GOALS 'SMART'!

SWOT ANALYSIS

The SWOT analysis is a super simple but effective tool to analyze your strengths. weaknesses, opportunities and threats. Use the space below to start analyzing yours!

STRENGTHS	WEAKNESSES
S	W
OPPORTUNITIES	**THREATS**
O	T

SECTION 3

BUDGET

WHY YOUR OLD BUDGET DIDN'T WORK

1. **It Wasn't Realistic**

If you are being too restrictive, your budget will not be sustainable. If you aren't being restrictive enough, your budget will not provide you with the boundaries to live within your means. While creating your budget (or spending plan, because a PLAN is really what it is), make sure you find the sweet spot between having enough funds to enjoy yourself (coffee, dinner, activities, etc.), but also having a hard "cap" or limit to avoid going crazy and overspending. Remember, the goal is **balance.** You will have to "give & take."

2. **It was too Restrictive**

Restrictive= Not Enjoyable.
No Fun= You Will Give Up.
Giving Up= Feeling Guilty.
Guilt= Shame.
Shame= You Will Never Get Ahead with Money.

3. **You Relied on Willpower Alone**

The easiest promise to break is the one you make with youself because there are (generally) no big consequences. Following through when it's just you vs. you is HARD. Set yourself up for success by not just relying on willpower alone. Plan ahead! Maybe it looks like having a certain amount of cash in your wallet, using a pre-paid card and only loading it on payday, or setting a boundary limit on your credit card.

"But isn't that restrictive?"

No, because you can give yourself plenty of funds to spend, but set a hard boundary to prevent overspending. Plan ahead for the road - blocks you know you'll face!

4. **You Let Finances Stress you Out Vs. Empower you**

If when you think about money and money management you get completely overwhelmed, you might need to sit down and unpack the reasons behind that. Although some think that money is the root of all evil, some also realize that money allows them to experience unique opportunities. There's no right or wrong answer, but the sooner you realize that money is not personally out to get you, the sooner you can start to enjoy the benefits that come with each transaction. When you have worked hard to save up to purchase that thing you've had your eye on, it feels SO GOOD. Learn to love the energy that comes with making big money moves.

5. **You Thought Each Month Looked the Same**

Sometimes it's easy to forget that a budget shouldn't look the same every single month. Some months you'll need to plan for higher spending (AKA Christmas season). If you fail to plan for these fluctuations, your budget will suffer. Don't forget things like your annual car registration, sprinkler blowouts or anything else that really only happens once per year.

"If you fail to plan, you plan to fail."

CREATING A SUCCESSFUL

BUDGET

STEPS	NOTES
Set Clear Financial Goals	
Tack your Income and Current Expenses	
Set Spending Limits & Prioritize Saving	
Be Flexible by Reviewing and Adjusting when Necessary	
Stay Disciplined and Create a Plan for When things get Hard	
Use Budgeting Tools and Seek Professional Help When Needed	
Plan for Debt Repayment When Necessary	
Celebrate Milestones, You've Earned It!	

SPENDING PLAN

*Starting:*____________________ *Ending:*____________________

HOME	AMOUNT
1 RENT/ MORTGAGE	$
2 HOME INSURANCE/HOA	$
3 UTILITIES (WATER, GAS, ELECTRIC)	$
4 TV & INTERNET	$
5 OUTDOOR/GARDEN	$
6 HOME REPAIRS	$
7	$
8	$
9	$

SPENDING PLAN

VEHICLE	AMOUNT
1 CAR PAYMENT	$
2 INSURANCE	$
3 GAS	$
4 MAINTENANCE	$
5	$
6	$
7	$
8	$
9	$

SPENDING PLAN

MEDICAL	AMOUNT
1 DOCTOR	$
2 DENTIST	$
3 EYESORE/CONTACTS	$
4 MEDICATION	$
5 SPA TREATMENT	$
6	$
7	$
8	$
9	$

SPENDING PLAN

FOOD	AMOUNT
1 GROCERIES	$
2 EATING OUT	$
3 FOOD SUBSCRIPTIONS	$
4 COFFEE	$
5	$
6	$
7	$
8	$
9	$

SPENDING PLAN

LIFE	AMOUNT
1 CHILD CARE/SUPPORT	$
2 BEAUTY/SKINCARE	$
3 CLOTHING	$
4 ENTERTAINMENT	$
5 GIFTS	$
6 SUBSCRIPTIONS	$
7	$
8	$
9	$

SPENDING PLAN

DEBT	AMOUNT
1 CREDIT CARD #1	$
2 CREDIT CARD #2	$
3 CREDIT CARD #3	$
4 STUDENT LOAN/ TUITION	$
5 LOAN #1	$
6 LOAN #2	$
7	$
8	$
9	$

OTHER

OTHER	AMOUNT
1	$
2	$
3	$
4	$
5	$

1 HOME TOTAL	$
2 VEHICLE TOTAL	$
3 MEDICAL TOTAL	$
4 FOOD TOTAL	$
5 LIFE TOTAL	$

BILL PAY

CHECKLIST

MONTH

BILL TO BE PAID:	J	F	M	A	M	J	J	A	S	O	N	D

BILL PAY

CHECKLIST

MONTH

BILL TO BE PAID:	J	F	M	A	M	J	J	A	S	O	N	D
	☐	☐	☐	☐	☐	☐	☐	☐	☐	☐	☐	☐
	☐	☐	☐	☐	☐	☐	☐	☐	☐	☐	☐	☐
	☐	☐	☐	☐	☐	☐	☐	☐	☐	☐	☐	☐
	☐	☐	☐	☐	☐	☐	☐	☐	☐	☐	☐	☐
	☐	☐	☐	☐	☐	☐	☐	☐	☐	☐	☐	☐
	☐	☐	☐	☐	☐	☐	☐	☐	☐	☐	☐	☐
	☐	☐	☐	☐	☐	☐	☐	☐	☐	☐	☐	☐
	☐	☐	☐	☐	☐	☐	☐	☐	☐	☐	☐	☐
	☐	☐	☐	☐	☐	☐	☐	☐	☐	☐	☐	☐
	☐	☐	☐	☐	☐	☐	☐	☐	☐	☐	☐	☐
	☐	☐	☐	☐	☐	☐	☐	☐	☐	☐	☐	☐
	☐	☐	☐	☐	☐	☐	☐	☐	☐	☐	☐	☐
	☐	☐	☐	☐	☐	☐	☐	☐	☐	☐	☐	☐
	☐	☐	☐	☐	☐	☐	☐	☐	☐	☐	☐	☐
	☐	☐	☐	☐	☐	☐	☐	☐	☐	☐	☐	☐
	☐	☐	☐	☐	☐	☐	☐	☐	☐	☐	☐	☐
	☐	☐	☐	☐	☐	☐	☐	☐	☐	☐	☐	☐
	☐	☐	☐	☐	☐	☐	☐	☐	☐	☐	☐	☐
	☐	☐	☐	☐	☐	☐	☐	☐	☐	☐	☐	☐

FINANCE LOG

By consistently documenting financial activities, a finance log provides valuable insights into spending patterns, aids in budgeting, and ensures that financial goals are on track.

DATE	ACCOUNT	WITHDRAWAL	DEPOSIT	BALANCE

FINANCE LOG

By consistently documenting financial activities, a finance log provides valuable insights into spending patterns, aids in budgeting, and ensures that financial goals are on track.

DATE	ACCOUNT	WITHDRAWAL	DEPOSIT	BALANCE

IRREGULAR EXPENSE

Not all expenses are the same each month. Things like vehicle registration, new tires or HOA bills come every once in a while. Keep track of irregular expenses here.

EXPENSE TO PLAN FOR	AMOUNT
1	$
2	$
3	$
4	$
5	$
6	$
7	$
8	$
9	$

DID YOU FIND A SURPRISE BILL YOU WEREN'T PLANNING FOR?

Keep an emergency fund as a safty net for those unplanned expenses.

AUTOMATED BILLS

Assure that you never miss an important payment (vehicle, home, credit card, etc.) by placing it on autopay. Keep track of the accounts you have on autopay here.

AUTOMATIC RENEWALS	AMOUNT
1	$
2	$
3	$
4	$
5	$
6	$
7	$
8	$
9	$

SUBSCRIPTIONS

Don't forget about the things you sign up for!

SUBSCRIPTIONS	AMOUNT
1	$
2	$
3	$
4	$
5	$
6	$
7	$
8	$
9	$

SECTION 4

SAVINGS

SAVINGS LOG

A savings log is essential for effective financial planning and achieving your savings goals. It acts as a visual record of your progress, helping you stay motivated and focused on building your savings.

DATE	ACCOUNT	WITHDRAWAL	DEPOSIT	BALANCE

SAVINGS LOG

DATE	ACCOUNT	WITHDRAWAL	DEPOSIT	BALANCE

CASH LOG

By keeping an accurate cash log, you can effectively manage your cash flow, detect discrepancies, and ensure financial integrity, contributing to better financial decision-making.

DATE	WITHDRAWAL	DEPOSIT	BALANCE	NOTES

CASH LOG

By keeping an accurate cash log, you can effectively manage your cash flow, detect discrepancies, and ensure financial integrity, contributing to better financial decision-making.

DATE	WITHDRAWAL	DEPOSIT	BALANCE	NOTES

RETIREMENT

Starting early with retirement planning enables you to take advantage of compounding interest, making your savings grow substantially over time!

EMPLOYER-SPONSORED RETIREMENT PLANS

Many employers offer retirement plans such as 401(k)s or 403(b)s. These plans allow you to contribute a portion of your pre-tax income, reducing your current taxable income. Employers may also match a percentage of your contributions, which is essentially "free" money for your retirement.

INDIVIDUAL RETIREMENT ACCOUNTS

IRAs are tax-advantaged accounts that individuals can open independently. There are two primary types: Traditional IRAs (with tax-deductible contributions but taxable withdrawals) and Roth IRAs (with after-tax contributions but tax-free withdrawals in retirement). Both offer advantages for retirement savings.

SELF EMPLOYED RETIREMENT PLANS

If you're self-employed or a small business owner, you have options like the Simplified Employee Pension (SEP) IRA or the Solo 401(k) to save for retirement while taking advantage of tax benefits.

TAXABLE INVESTMENT ACCOUNTS

While retirement accounts offer tax advantages, you can also invest in taxable brokerage accounts. These accounts provide flexibility in terms of investments and withdrawal timing but lack the tax advantages of retirement accounts.

HEALTH SAVINGS ACCOUNT

If you have a high-deductible health plan, you can contribute to an HSA. While primarily designed for medical expenses, HSAs offer tax benefits, and after age 65, you can withdraw funds for non-medical expenses penalty-free, making it a potential retirement savings vehicle.

REAL ESTATE/ RENTAL INCOME

Owning real estate properties, such as rental properties or real estate investment trusts (REITs), can generate rental income, which can be a source of retirement income. Real estate can also appreciate over time, providing a potential source of wealth.

RETIREMENT

Make note of the accounts you have, or those you feel might be a good fit for you.

EMPLOYER-SPONSORED RETIREMENT PLANS	INDIVIDUAL RETIREMENT ACCOUNTS	SELF EMPLOYED RETIREMENT PLANS

TAXABLE INVESTMENT ACCOUNTS	HEALTH SAVINGS ACCOUNT	REAL ESTATE/ RENTAL INCOME

EMERGENCY FUNDS

An emergency fund is a financial safety net that individuals and households set up to cover unexpected expenses or financial emergencies. It provides peace of mind and financial security, as it helps you avoid going into debt or using credit cards when unexpected financial crises occur, such as medical bills, car repairs, job loss, or home repairs. Having an emergency fund in place can help you maintain financial stability and stay on track with your long-term financial goals.

EMERGENCY CASH	EMERGENCY SAVINGS ACCOUNT	OTHER

NOTES:

PROGRESS TRACKER

Use this chart to track how close you are to obtaining your savings goal.

GOAL:

DEADLINE:

DATE	0%	20%	60%	80%	100%

Check in with yourself every few weeks/months to assure you're making progress.

PROGRESS TRACKER

GOAL:

DEADLINE:

DATE	0%	20%	60%	80%	100%

Check in with yourself every few weeks/months to assure you're making progress.

SECTION 5

DEBT

DEBT PRIORITY

DEBT	PRIORITY (LEAST → GREATEST)
____________________	0 1 2 3 4 5 6 7 8 9 10
____________________	0 1 2 3 4 5 6 7 8 9 10
____________________	0 1 2 3 4 5 6 7 8 9 10
____________________	0 1 2 3 4 5 6 7 8 9 10
____________________	0 1 2 3 4 5 6 7 8 9 10
____________________	0 1 2 3 4 5 6 7 8 9 10
____________________	0 1 2 3 4 5 6 7 8 9 10
____________________	0 1 2 3 4 5 6 7 8 9 10

DEBT PRIORITY

DEBT	PRIORITY
	LEAST … GREATEST
____________________	0 1 2 3 4 5 6 7 8 9 10
____________________	0 1 2 3 4 5 6 7 8 9 10
____________________	0 1 2 3 4 5 6 7 8 9 10
____________________	0 1 2 3 4 5 6 7 8 9 10

MAKING SENSE OF YOUR SCORES

0-3 It made the list, but you aren't starting here.

4-7 You'll keep it in mind, but you may only work on it here-or-there.

8-10 You should focus all of your energy here first!

CREDIT CARD TRACKER

CREDIT CARD:

PAYMENT AMOUNT:

TOTAL CREDIT LIMIT:

TOTAL OWED:

PAY OFF PROGRESS	0%	20%	60%	80%	100%
Date:					
Date:					
Date:					
Date:					
Date:					
Date:					
Date:					

CREDIT CARD TRACKER

CREDIT CARD:

PAYMENT AMOUNT:

TOTAL CREDIT LIMIT:

TOTAL OWED:

PAY OFF PROGRESS	0%	20%	60%	80%	100%
Date:					
Date:					
Date:					
Date:					
Date:					
Date:					
Date:					

CREDIT CARD TRACKER

CREDIT CARD:

PAYMENT AMOUNT:

TOTAL CREDIT LIMIT:

TOTAL OWED:

PAY OFF PROGRESS	0%	20%	60%	80%	100%
Date:					
Date:					
Date:					
Date:					
Date:					
Date:					
Date:					

CREDIT CARD TRACKER

CREDIT CARD:	PAYMENT AMOUNT:
TOTAL CREDIT LIMIT:	TOTAL OWED:

PAY OFF PROGRESS	0%	20%	60%	80%	100%
Date:					
Date:					
Date:					
Date:					
Date:					
Date:					
Date:					

INSTALLMENT CREDIT

LOAN TRACKER

LOAN:

PAYMENT AMOUNT:

TOTAL LOAN AMOUNT:

TOTAL OWED:

PAY OFF PROGRESS	0%	20%	60%	80%	100%
Date:					
Date:					
Date:					
Date:					
Date:					
Date:					
Date:					

LOAN TRACKER

LOAN:	PAYMENT AMOUNT:
TOTAL LOAN AMOUNT:	TOTAL OWED:

PAY OFF PROGRESS 0% 20% 60% 80% 100%

Date:

Date:

Date:

Date:

Date:

Date:

Date:

LOAN TRACKER

LOAN:	PAYMENT AMOUNT:
TOTAL LOAN AMOUNT:	TOTAL OWED:

PAY OFF PROGRESS	0%	20%	60%	80%	100%
Date:					
Date:					
Date:					
Date:					
Date:					
Date:					
Date:					

LOAN TRACKER

LOAN:

PAYMENT AMOUNT:

TOTAL LOAN AMOUNT:

TOTAL OWED:

PAY OFF PROGRESS	0%	20%	60%	80%	100%
Date:					
Date:					
Date:					
Date:					
Date:					
Date:					
Date:					

INSTALLMENT CREDIT

LOAN TRACKER

LOAN:

PAYMENT AMOUNT:

TOTAL LOAN AMOUNT:

TOTAL OWED:

PAY OFF PROGRESS	0%	20%	60%	80%	100%
Date:					
Date:					
Date:					
Date:					
Date:					
Date:					
Date:					

SECTION 6

OTHER

PASSWORDS

USERNAME PASSWORD

WEEKLY MEAL GUIDE

WEEK OF:

SUNDAY

MONDAY

TUESDAY

WEDNESDAY

THURSDAY

FRIDAY

SATURDAY

NOTES

WEEKLY MEAL GUIDE

WEEK OF:

SUNDAY

MONDAY

TUESDAY

WEDNESDAY

THURSDAY

FRIDAY

SATURDAY

NOTES

WEEKLY MEAL GUIDE

WEEK OF:

SUNDAY

MONDAY

TUESDAY

WEDNESDAY

THURSDAY

FRIDAY

SATURDAY

NOTES

WEEKLY MEAL GUIDE

WEEK OF:

SUNDAY

MONDAY

TUESDAY

WEDNESDAY

THURSDAY

FRIDAY

SATURDAY

NOTES

GROCERY LIST

WEEK OF:

PRODUCE

DELI

MEAT/PROTEIN

CANNED GOODS

DAIRY

BAKERY

FROZEN GOODS

OTHER

GROCERY LIST

BEVERAGES

SNACKS

BAKING SUPPLIES

HOUSEHOLD

PHARMACY

PERSONAL CARE

PET

OTHER

GROCERY LIST

WEEK OF:

PRODUCE

DELI

MEAT/PROTEIN

CANNED GOODS

DAIRY

BAKERY

FROZEN GOODS

OTHER

GROCERY LIST

BEVERAGES

SNACKS

BAKING SUPPLIES

HOUSEHOLD

PHARMACY

PERSONAL CARE

PET

OTHER

NOTES

NOTES

DAILY PLANNER

TODAY'S PRIORITIES

1
2
3

DATE:

TODAYS SCHEDULE

8:00 AM
9:00 AM
10:00 AM
11:00 AM
12:00 PM
1:00 PM
2:00 PM
3:00 PM
4:00 PM
5:00 PM
6:00 PM
6:00 PM

IMPORTANT REMINDERS

MEALS OF THE DAY

BREAKFAST
LUNCH
DINNER

NOTES

DAILY PLANNER

TODAY'S PRIORITIES

1.
2.
3.

TODAYS SCHEDULE

8:00 AM

9:00 AM

10:00 AM

11:00 AM

12:00 PM

1:00 PM

2:00 PM

3:00 PM

4:00 PM

5:00 PM

6:00 PM

6:00 PM

DATE:

IMPORTANT REMINDERS

MEALS OF THE DAY

BREAKFAST

LUNCH

DINNER

NOTES

DAILY PLANNER

TODAY'S PRIORITIES

1
2
3

DATE:

IMPORTANT REMINDERS

TODAYS SCHEDULE

8:00 AM
9:00 AM
10:00 AM
11:00 AM
12:00 PM
1:00 PM
2:00 PM
3:00 PM
4:00 PM
5:00 PM
6:00 PM
6:00 PM

MEALS OF THE DAY

BREAKFAST
LUNCH
DINNER

NOTES

DAILY PLANNER

TODAY'S PRIORITIES

1.
2.
3.

DATE:

IMPORTANT REMINDERS

TODAYS SCHEDULE

8:00 AM

9:00 AM

10:00 AM

11:00 AM

12:00 PM

1:00 PM

2:00 PM

3:00 PM

4:00 PM

5:00 PM

6:00 PM

6:00 PM

MEALS OF THE DAY

BREAKFAST

LUNCH

DINNER

NOTES

DAILY PLANNER

TODAY'S PRIORITIES

1
2
3

DATE:

IMPORTANT REMINDERS

TODAYS SCHEDULE

8:00 AM
9:00 AM
10:00 AM
11:00 AM
12:00 PM
1:00 PM
2:00 PM
3:00 PM
4:00 PM
5:00 PM
6:00 PM
6:00 PM

MEALS OF THE DAY

BREAKFAST
LUNCH
DINNER

NOTES

DAILY PLANNER

TODAY'S PRIORITIES

1.
2.
3.

DATE:

IMPORTANT REMINDERS

TODAYS SCHEDULE

8:00 AM

9:00 AM

10:00 AM

11:00 AM

12:00 PM

1:00 PM

2:00 PM

3:00 PM

4:00 PM

5:00 PM

6:00 PM

6:00 PM

MEALS OF THE DAY

BREAKFAST

LUNCH

DINNER

NOTES

DAILY PLANNER

TODAY'S PRIORITIES

1
2
3

DATE:

IMPORTANT REMINDERS

TODAYS SCHEDULE

8:00 AM

9:00 AM

10:00 AM

11:00 AM

12:00 PM

1:00 PM

2:00 PM

3:00 PM

4:00 PM

5:00 PM

6:00 PM

6:00 PM

MEALS OF THE DAY

BREAKFAST

LUNCH

DINNER

NOTES

DAILY PLANNER

TODAY'S PRIORITIES

1.
2.
3.

DATE:

IMPORTANT REMINDERS

TODAYS SCHEDULE

8:00 AM

9:00 AM

10:00 AM

11:00 AM

12:00 PM

1:00 PM

2:00 PM

3:00 PM

4:00 PM

5:00 PM

6:00 PM

6:00 PM

MEALS OF THE DAY

BREAKFAST

LUNCH

DINNER

NOTES

DAILY PLANNER

TODAY'S PRIORITIES

1
2
3

DATE:

IMPORTANT REMINDERS

TODAYS SCHEDULE

8:00 AM
9:00 AM
10:00 AM
11:00 AM
12:00 PM
1:00 PM
2:00 PM
3:00 PM
4:00 PM
5:00 PM
6:00 PM
6:00 PM

MEALS OF THE DAY

BREAKFAST
LUNCH
DINNER

NOTES

DAILY PLANNER

TODAY'S PRIORITIES

1
2
3

DATE:

TODAYS SCHEDULE

8:00 AM

9:00 AM

10:00 AM

11:00 AM

12:00 PM

1:00 PM

2:00 PM

3:00 PM

4:00 PM

5:00 PM

6:00 PM

6:00 PM

IMPORTANT REMINDERS

MEALS OF THE DAY

BREAKFAST

LUNCH

DINNER

NOTES

DAILY PLANNER

TODAY'S PRIORITIES

1
2
3

TODAYS SCHEDULE

8:00 AM
9:00 AM
10:00 AM
11:00 AM
12:00 PM
1:00 PM
2:00 PM
3:00 PM
4:00 PM
5:00 PM
6:00 PM
6:00 PM

DATE:

IMPORTANT REMINDERS

MEALS OF THE DAY

BREAKFAST
LUNCH
DINNER

NOTES

DAILY PLANNER

TODAY'S PRIORITIES

1.
2.
3.

DATE:

IMPORTANT REMINDERS

TODAYS SCHEDULE

8:00 AM

9:00 AM

10:00 AM

11:00 AM

12:00 PM

1:00 PM

2:00 PM

3:00 PM

4:00 PM

5:00 PM

6:00 PM

6:00 PM

MEALS OF THE DAY

BREAKFAST

LUNCH

DINNER

NOTES

DAILY PLANNER

TODAY'S PRIORITIES

1.
2.
3.

DATE:

IMPORTANT REMINDERS

TODAYS SCHEDULE

8:00 AM

9:00 AM

10:00 AM

11:00 AM

12:00 PM

1:00 PM

2:00 PM

3:00 PM

4:00 PM

5:00 PM

6:00 PM

6:00 PM

MEALS OF THE DAY

BREAKFAST

LUNCH

DINNER

NOTES

DAILY PLANNER

TODAY'S PRIORITIES

1.
2.
3.

DATE: ....

IMPORTANT REMINDERS

TODAYS SCHEDULE

8:00 AM

9:00 AM

10:00 AM

11:00 AM

12:00 PM

1:00 PM

2:00 PM

3:00 PM

4:00 PM

5:00 PM

6:00 PM

6:00 PM

MEALS OF THE DAY

BREAKFAST

LUNCH

DINNER

NOTES

YOUR

FEEDBACK

IS IMPORTANT

Take a photo of your answers and send them to @JennaaStillman on Instagram or email them to Jennaastillman@gmail.com to receive a free digital gift!

Did you enjoy this book? We loved it! As expected Not really

How would you rate the templates provided? 1 2 3 4 5

What did you most like about this book?

How likely are you to recommend us to your family & friends?

unlikely 0 1 2 3 4 5 6 7 8 9 10 Definitely!

How would you rate the educational content?

Poor Fair Acceptable Good Excellent

If you have any other comments or suggestions, we would love to hear them below!

THANK YOU FOR YOUR FEEDBACK!

☆☆☆☆☆

"Overall, your budgeting workbook has become an indispensable tool in my financial journey. I can't thank you enough for creating such a valuable resource and for your ongoing support and guidance. I'm excited to continue using it and seeing the positive impact it has on my financial well-being."

REVIEW FROM NATASHA PALACIOS

09/26/23

☆☆☆☆☆

"Your workbook's practical exercises, education, and templates are incredibly helpful and have made the process of budgeting feel less overwhelming. This book is relevant for everyone, regardless of their income or financial goals."

REVIEW FROM JAYLYNN GIDDENS

01/01/23

WE HOPE YOU ENJOYED THIS WORKBOOK!

BUDGETING FOR BEGINNERS

BY JENNA STILLMAN

GET IN TOUCH

@JENNAASTILLMAN

JENNAASTILLMAN@GMAIL.COM

Made in United States
Orlando, FL
04 November 2026

90218653R00061

DISCOVER THE SECRET TO A BETTER FINANCIAL LIF

Keep all of your financial information organized with this easy-to-use budgeting workbook. Each section is specially designed for your uniq lifestyle, and will help you quickly achieve your goals!

In this workbook, you can find:

-Specific goal setting
-Monthly budgeting templates
-Bill pay checklist
-Expense tracker
-Automatic subscription tracker
-Saving trackers (including emergency and retirement)
-Bill pay-off tracker
-Shopping list
-Much, much more!

ISBN 9781737523123
90000
9 781737 523123